M000286885

**BY RICHARD
DE LA MORA**

—

14 WAYS TO
KEEP YOUR
LOVE FRESH
FOR HER

**14 VIDEOS
INCLUDED**

SEE HOW TO
WATCH INSIDE

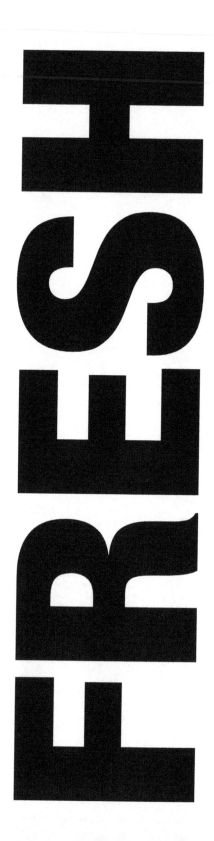

FRESH
FRESH

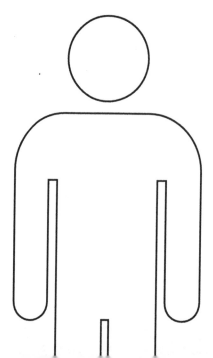

Copyright © 2018 Fireproof Ministries

All rights reserved. No portion of this book may be reproduced, stored in a retrieval system, or transmitted in any form or by any means—electronic, mechanical, photocopy, recording, scanning, or other—except for brief quotations in critical reviews or articles, without the prior written permission of the publisher. Published in Pasadena, CA by Fireproof Ministries. Fireproof Ministries titles may be purchased in bulk for educational, business, fundraising, or sales promotional use. For information, please e-mail **info@ fireproofministries.com**.

Unless otherwise noted, Scriptures are taken from the New International Version®, NIV®, The Message, New Living Translation, New King James Version, and The English Standard Version, New American Standard Bible, King James Version. Copyright © 1973, 1978, 1984, 2011 by Biblica, Inc.™ Used by permission from Zondervan. All rights reserved worldwide.

www.zondervan.com.

The Library of Congress Cataloging-in-Publication

Data is on file with the Library of Congress

ISBN-13: 978-0692997604

Contents

How to get the most out of this book

Don't you just love the feeling of buying something new? For instance, when you get a new car, a new pair of shoes, or a new outfit? There's nothing like the excitement that comes from getting something new. We designed this book to create that kind of feeling in you and your significant other. There is an old saying that when you get into a relationship, the excitement stops there, but we believe when you get into a relationship it only gets better.

This book will reignite the fire and passion in your relationship. What you are saying by taking on this 14-day challenge with us is that keeping the flame of love burning within your relationship matters. You don't get a fire simply because you want one, you get a fire because you create one. This challenge will create that fire. This book was designed to ensure that not only will the fire in your relationship with your partner grow, but the fire in your relationship with God will grow as well.

We have written this book for those who are dating, engaged and even for those whom are married. This book is meant to be a 14-day challenge; however, we understand that if you are dating you may not see each other daily. So, feel free to take as long as you need with this book. Something you may notice about the two different books is the chapter titles and challenges are the same. The challenges are the same, because we want you to do them together. However, the content is different because Britt wrote from her perspective to the women and I wrote from my perspective to the men. In the future, if the two of you want to take this 14-day challenge again, we encourage you to do so. You could even switch books to get a completely different perspective. We believe God will speak to you differently every time you read this book because as time passes and new experiences come your way, your outlook will change. We encourage you take this challenge once a year to keep the fire in your relationship or marriage burning. We are so excited for what God is going to do in your lives and we pray that your relationship will always remain fresh and on fire.

This book follows along with the 14 videos created by Rich and Britt. Please send an email to **14days@strongermarriages.com** and we will send you a link to access the video series. If you have any issue reach out to us at **info@ strongermarriages.com**.

Thanks,
Rich and Britt

—

CHAPTER ONE

Dream on Purpose

C.S Lewis once said, *"You are never too old to set another goal or to dream a new dream."* I believe dreams are the heartbeat of any relationship and once you lose your dream, you lose the beat of your relationship. Your dream is what gives your relationship drive. It gives you fire for your day and reminds you of what you're working to accomplish together. Dreams matter because dreams are consistently creating a new future.

My wife and I continually dream on purpose. At the end of every year, we celebrate what we have accomplished, but we don't stay stuck on our past victories because there are more dreams to be accomplished. Then at the beginning of each year, we write new dreams. We ask God to stir us up and give us new dreams. New dreams that will help others and glorify Him. We ask for new dreams that will leave behind a legacy, and that will challenge our relationship. We are dreamers, and if dreaming is free, then we should do more of it.

When I think of a dreamer in the Bible, Joseph is the first one who comes to mind. Genesis 37:9 teaches us that Joseph dreamt again. I love this about Joseph because he always had a dream in his heart, it never left him. I believe that just as Joseph dreamt again, we should do the same for our relationship. We should always have a dream in our heart and a dream for our relationship. Joseph held onto his dream and even when life hit him, it didn't affect him because he knew what he was working towards. Do you know what you're working to accomplish? Do you have a dream that drives you?

When my wife and I talk to couples who are going through hard times, one of the first questions I'll ask is, *"What are your dreams, what are you striving toward?"* I've realized the couples who have lost their dream, have also lost their hope in their relationship because they have no purpose together. They have nothing to get them going. They live life wandering, rather than walking life purposefully, all because of the absence of a dream. That's why I'm encouraging you to dream on purpose.

When Brittni and I come together, and we figure out our dreams for the year, we make sure our decisions are in alignment with our dreams. Here's a reminder, your dreams and your vision must line up with your decisions. If the decision doesn't match your dreams and vision, then don't do it. A couple who isn't mindful of their steps, is a couple who isn't mindful of their dreams. Are you mindful of your dreams? If so, are you allowing your decisions to line up with your dreams? Friend, never stop dreaming, and most of all never allow anyone or anything interfere with your dreams.

Today, it's time to revive the fire in your relationship. My wife and I challenge you to dream on purpose with your partner. Pray and take as much time as you need to create a vision for your future. Write down your goals on the pages we have provided along with a plan of attack. What does the future of your relationship look like and what steps will you take to get there?

Journal below:

Write what you learned today, how it went and
what memories were made.

CHAPTER TWO

—

Break the Routine

"Will you have another Americano today?" I get asked this question by the barista every time I walk into my local Starbucks. The reason he asks me this question is because I have a routine. I am a firm believer in, *"If it's not broke, don't fix it."* There is no problem with having a routine. However, there is a problem when your love life is routine because what once may have won your partner's attention doesn't ensure that it will forever keep their attention. We must learn to break the routine.

When you break the routine, you break away from familiarity. If there is one thing that will destroy a relationship-it's familiarity. The Bible teaches us that Jesus couldn't do many miracles in his hometown because the people were familiar with him. Their familiarity hindered their miracles because they no longer had an expectation. Could the reason why your love life might need a miracle is because things have become too familiar?

Here's what familiarity does: It will get you to value others more than you value your partner. Familiarity will get you to find excitement with things other than your relationship. Familiarity will get you to grow comfortable with each other. Comfort is the enemy of growth. If you aren't growing, then your relationship is slowly dying, that's why we need to break the routine.

So, what does it look like to break the routine? Instead of going to the same restaurant every weekend, go to a place that the two of you have never been. Instead of buying her the occasional flowers for a special occasion, write her a letter, or leave her a note on the mirror before she wakes up. Do something she's always wanted you to do, but you never had the time for. Breaking the routine doesn't need to be extravagant, as long as it's heartfelt.

It's time to freshen up your relationship! My wife and I challenge you and your partner to break the routine. Use some of the examples I provided in the paragraph above, or come up with something exciting and heartfelt on your own. Do something unexpected. Your wife, or wife-to-be, will appreciate the surprise romantic gesture more than you know. Journal about your experience below and remember that breaking the routine should become a part of your routine.

Journal below:

Write what you learned today, how it went and
what memories were made.

CHAPTER THREE

Declare It

If there is one thing I admire most about my mother, it would be her relentless faith. When my mother is sure of something, you cannot talk her out of it. She will stand on the Word, and she will declare the Word. She is relentless. I will never forget my mom's former declaration. Day after day she would declare that one day her son would become a preacher. When she would say this, I didn't believe her because that was not what I wanted to do with my life. I had other things in mind. I wanted to be a music producer, but God had other plans. What I love about my mom is that my circumstances never changed her declaration, but her declaration changed my circumstances. I went from producing music to seeking Jesus and eventually became a preacher. My life changed drastically for the better because of one woman's bold declaration.

Imagine what would happen if we learned to declare God's promises over our relationships. I wonder what things would drastically change if we stood on and declared the Word of God. God knows the power of our words. You can see this throughout the Scriptures. In the book of Genesis, when God wanted to form something, He would speak it out; and whatever He said, came to fruition. Genesis is a reminder to us that our harvest relies on our seed. If you want to change the harvest, then you must change the seed. If you want to change the circumstance, then you must change the declaration. Just imagine if you began declaring life over your relationship. I wonder what blessings would flow into your lives.

What the enemy wants to do to our relationships is to sow a seed of division. The enemy knows that what's in unity receives God's commanded blessing, but what is divided cannot stand. Therefore, he tries to break up your words, because if he can breakup your words, then he can breakup your harvest. Proverbs 18:21 teaches us that the power of life and death are on the tongue. You have power on your tongue, but what are you going to do with that power? You're either going to allow your relationship to be powerful or powerless, it all depends on what you're declaring. What I love to do throughout my day is declare the word of God over my life and my family's life. I have learned that my expectations come from my declarations. If I want to see something come to pass, then I need my words to line up with what I desire. Question, are your words lining up with what you desire? You can't put in a wrong address and expect to arrive at the right destination. Are your words leading your relationship to where you want to go? Or are they leading you astray?

Friends, just like my mother declared what she wanted to see over my life, we must do the same, because our words can change the trajectory of relationships. My wife and I challenge you to fast from all negative talk for the remainder of this book. The challenge is that you will not allow words to come out of your mouth that are not in alignment with the Word of God. We want each of you to select a Scripture that you can declare over your circumstances. We believe that as you do this, your circumstances will come into alignment with the Word of God. Be sure to journal down the circumstances that you want to see a change in and write down the Scripture that you will be declaring over them. Brittni and I pray God's favor and blessing over your lives. Have fun with this challenge.

Journal below:

Write what you learned today, how it went and
what memories were made.

—

CHAPTER FOUR

Intentional Devotionals

Since being married to my wife Brittni, I have learned a few things about her. Number one, never wake her when she is sleeping, unless you want to encounter the dark side of her. Number two, never interrupt her while she is spending time with God. In our household, spending time with God is non-negotiable because we know it's God who brought us together and it's God who will keep us together. Therefore, we are intentional when it comes to our devotion time. The word intentional means you're doing something on purpose. In other words, if you go the gym, you intend to stay fit, if you go to the grocery store, you intend to buy food, and when you hang out with God, you intend to grow in Him. Many people want their relationship to be on fire for God, but they aren't around God enough for their relationship to catch on fire.

I'll never forget when I went camping with my family. My dad warned us not to put our shoes close to the fire pit because they would burn. Did we listen? No. Instead we put our shoes close to the fire pit, and they started to burn. When our shoes weren't close to the fire, they were fine. It was only when our shoes were too close that they were affected by the fire. The same is true in our walks with God, if we aren't in the presence of God, our relationships cool off. When we are in His presence often, that's when our relationship catches on fire for Him. That's why we need to be intentional about meeting with God.

One of my favorite life verses is Matthew 6:33 (ESV). It says, *"But seek first the kingdom of God and His righteousness, and all these things shall be added to you."* This text is a beautiful reminder that when we seek God, He adds to our lives. He adds wisdom to our lives, He adds peace to our lives, and gives us strength for our day. However, this only happens when we first seek Him. Could the reason God isn't adding to your life is that you aren't adding God to your everyday life? We shouldn't work God into our schedules; we should work our schedules around God.

Britt and I asked a good friend of ours, *"When do you read the Bible?"* She responded, *"I read it at the end of the day, before bed, because it gives me peace and puts my mind at rest."* What I found interesting about our friend's logic was that even though she was going through trials, she felt the need to put God at the end of her day rather than at the beginning of her day. Imagine if she would have put God before her battles and not at the end of her battles. If only she had put God at the beginning of her day, He could have given her the wisdom, joy, and peace she needed to combat her battles. Instead, she faced her battles each day without a word from God. Therefore, it is imperative for us to seek God every morning. I have realized the enemy does not want you to be intentional with your devotionals, he would rather you be occasional with your devotionals.

Today, my wife and I encourage you to be intentional with your morning devotionals. We challenge you to seek God before you seek each other. After seeking God, connect with your partner about how God spoke to each of you in your time of study and prayer. Remember, as you first seek God, not only will all your needs be provided for, but your love for Him will grow as well. As your love for God grows, so will your love for each other. Make sure to journal about your experience and have a blessed time with God.

Journal below:

Write what you learned today, how it went and
what memories were made.

—

CHAPTER FIVE

Build the Bridge to Communication

If there is one thing that will hinder your relationship, it is lack of communication. Communication is a necessary bridge in every relationship. Without a healthy communication bridge, you will find it difficult to resolve any problem that may arise. When you don't communicate effectively, you don't build bridges, you burn bridges. The devil's assignment is to burn the bridge to communication.

In our first year of marriage, one of our greatest struggles was communication. The reason for this is because Brittni and I speak in two different languages. When I speak, she often doesn't want the short version of my answer; she wants the long version. However, when she speaks, I don't want the long version, I want the short version. I just want her to tell me specifically what she needs, so that I can run with it. The problem with this is if I don't learn her language, then I can't communicate effectively with her.

In Genesis chapter 11 when everyone had the same language, they were able to build effectively. But the moment God confused their language, they could no longer build. I know this passage refers to God confusing their language because they wanted to build their name rather than His. However, there is wisdom to reap from this passage. When you're in unison with your speech, there isn't a goal you cannot reach. Most goals lay by the wayside because of misplaced communication.

James 1:19 (NLT) teaches us, "*Be quick to listen, slow to speak, and slow to get angry.*" The first thing we need to do to improve our communication is be quick to listen. What does this mean? Exactly what it says, "*Be quick to listen.*" In other words, it doesn't mean to give advice or to interrupt; it simply means to listen. You won't know what your partner is going through if you don't take the time to listen to her. You'll never know how to solve the problem when you don't know what the problem is. When you're all ears, what you're communicating to her is, "*I value you.*" When you're all mouth, what you are communicating is, "*It's all about me.*" The second thing this Scripture teaches us is to be slow to speak. In other words, when you listen, and you know the problem, ask God for wisdom to help you communicate. What we often do wrong is speak, then pray, rather than pray then speak. When you pray before you speak, you won't be emotionally led; you will be spiritually led. When you are spiritually led, you build bridges rather than burn bridges. The last thing this Scripture teaches us is to be slow to get angry. Why be slow to get angry? Because learning the truth and walking in humility is not easy. We may get a response that challenges our flesh, but to build a strong bridge to communication, we need to be patient with one another.

Today, my wife and I challenge you to have a conversation with your partner about how you can effectively build the bridge to communication. Discuss how the different Scriptures we have given you speak to you, and how you will apply them to your everyday life. My wife has provided two different Scriptures for your lady, but go ahead and write all of them down. Next, we would like for both of you to post them on the refrigerator, or on your desk so you can continue to meditate on them. The next time one of you is misunderstanding one another, or a disagreement arises, remember what you learned today and use these Scriptures to lead you both to a solution. Be sure to journal about how this conversation has helped you grow today.

Journal below:

Write what you learned today, how it went and
what memories were made.

—

CHAPTER SIX

To Serve Not to Be Served

People have asked me what quality in Brittni I find most attractive. Yes, I'm attracted to her beauty, yes I am attracted to the love she has for Jesus, but the way she serves people gets me going. To this day, you will find her passionately serving in the house of God, helping women who are in the adult industry and serving our community. Her service is attractive to me because people who are servants aren't selfish; they are selfless. Selfish people see through the lens of me, people who serve see through the lens of we. I truly believe the reason why relationships have lost their flame is that they became consumed with themselves. If you aren't careful, your conversations will consist of finger-pointing. *"This is what you can do better. Why are or aren't you like this?"* The problem with this is that we fail to look in the mirror to realize that we've become self-indulgent. Before we move forward, it's not a bad idea to lovingly confront your partner, but if you only confront her without confronting yourself, then you won't create change, you just create a new way to complain.

There is a woman in the Bible who was known for complaining and for her bitterness, her name was Naomi. She had a valid reason to complain. She had lost her husband and her two sons. I can't imagine what it would be like to be in her shoes. She lost the ones who were dearest to her heart. Her loss affected her so much she wanted to change her name from Naomi to Marah, which means bitterness. Her bitterness was slowly consuming her life until her daughter in law, Ruth, intervened. The Bible teaches us that Boaz noticed Ruth while she was out gleaning the field. The Scripture says Boaz ordered his servants to leave behind extra grain in the fields so he could bless Ruth with more. He did this because he was attracted to her. When Ruth returned home to Naomi with extra grain, Naomi asked her where she had gleaned and who took notice of her because she had more than a fair share of grain. Ruth explained to her that she was in a field that belonged to Boaz. Naomi quickly began the role of a matchmaker being that Boaz was a relative of hers. Her advice to Ruth was what was needed to make Boaz and Ruth a couple. The two of them got married and bore a son. What I find astounding about this is that the moment Naomi took her eyes off herself, she went from bitter to better. She was better because she stopped thinking about herself. What would happen in your relationship if you took your eyes off yourself and placed them on other people? God would move in your life as he did in

Naomi's life. Naomi got her fire for life back because she helped somebody else get their fire back. In other words, you reap what you sow. What you sow into other relationships, you will reap in your own relationship. My wife and I find this to be true; nearly every day, we sow into the lives of others, and in return, God sows into our lives because there is power in serving.

Today, my wife and I challenge you and your partner to have an honest discussion about serving. Do you currently serve? Do you serve in a church, in your community, and in your household? If so, how have you seen God move in your life through your acts of service? If you don't currently serve, we challenge you both to serve together in your local church or community. When you give back to God's people, He will give back to you. Serving others will grow you as a couple, and as you plant yourself in God's house through serving, you will begin to flourish. Be sure to journal about this topic of conversation and mark your next date of service on your calendar. Also, we want to see you in action! Snap a photo of you and your lady serving and post it on Instagram or Facebook with the hashtag #14daychallenge for a potential repost.

Journal below:

Write what you learned today, how it went and
what memories were made.

CHAPTER SEVEN

—

Pause for Celebration

The other day I was with a friend of mine, and we were trying to get to Los Angeles. I was so hungry that morning, so we pulled off the highway and went to a drive-thru to save time. We pulled up, placed our order, and then paid at the next window. The teller told us to drive forward to the next window to pick up our food. Being the wise man that I am, instead of pulling up to the window and grabbing our food, I kept driving straight towards the freeway. My friend looked at me and said, *"Rich, where are you going?"* I replied, *"Los Angeles?"* He then responded and said, *"You paid the lady, but you forgot our food!"* I replied, *"Oh no, you're right!"* I was so embarrassed because I didn't know where my mind was. I pulled over and went back to grab our food. As the employee gave me our food, she and all the employees started laughing. I began to wonder how many times we find ourselves going through the motions that we lose sight of the enjoyment. We get so caught up in conquering our mountains as a couple that we never take time to celebrate the view. That's why I want to encourage you to pause for celebration.

What I admire about God is that He consistently teaches us to pause for celebration. We notice this Genesis 1:31 (NKJV), *"Then God saw everything that He had made, and indeed it was very good. So, the evening and the morning were the sixth day."*

You'll notice that God has a pattern when creating. First He created, then He celebrated. When He created, He didn't keep creating more. Instead, He created and then He celebrated. Why? Because conquering a destination without celebration doesn't give glory to God and doesn't motivate you to keep going. Therefore, I encourage you to pause for celebration. The moment that you and your lady conquer a goal, celebrate. The moment you and your lady get a breakthrough, celebrate. The moment you and your lady don't argue over things you would usually argue over, celebrate. The moment your wife doesn't spend a lot of money on shopping, celebrate. If there's anything to celebrate, do it. My prayer for you is that you don't live life going through the motions so much so that you fail to enjoy life.

Here's what Solomon recommends, *"So I recommend having fun, because there is nothing better for people in this world than to eat, drink, and enjoy life."* Ecclesiastes 8:15 (NLT)

Today, my wife and I challenge you and your partner to rejoice and pause for celebration. We would like for the two of you to create a list of the progress you have made together. Once you have completed this list, we want you to celebrate this progress by thanking God for how far you have come. Then we want you to encourage one another. Tell your partner how proud of her you are. Remind her that you are fighting together and that her dreams matter to you. Remind her that she is not alone and that as a team the two of you will conquer your goals. Lastly, we want you to praise God for what He has already done. Thank Him because He knows the end from the beginning. You may only be at the beginning, but God already has an ending in mind. So, thank Him because as you rejoice in Him, He will give you the desires of your heart. Be sure to journal about your experience and remember, the best is yet to come.

Journal below:

Write what you learned today, how it went and what memories were made.

—

CHAPTER EIGHT

Disconnect from What's Disconnecting You

If there is one thing that's great about my millennial generation, it is that we are a social media-driven. Because of this, it means that at the tip of our fingers, we have access to information quicker than we ever have, in an instant we can stay updated on people's personal everyday lives, and we can get to know people quicker than ever. One major issue with this is we know how to facetime on the phone, but we have forgotten the value of facetime in person. We can connect on the phone but we are unable to connect in person. The disconnect happens because you cannot translate emotion and you cannot transfer your presence. Have you ever texted someone and had them completely misinterpret what you said? This kind of thing is known to cause arguments and disagreements because they perceived what you said to be hurtful when in actuality that was never your intention. How does this happen? It happens because you can't see a persons emotions nor hear the tone of their voice. Because you don't have an accurate interpretation of their feelings, your assumption creates a conflict and the conflict creates a disconnect. We need to learn to disconnect from what is disconnecting us.

I love what Proverbs 4:25 (MSG) says, *"Keep your eyes straight ahead: ignore all sideshow distractions."* In other words, in our everyday lives, we need to learn to keep our relationships in focus by ignoring anything that has the potential to distract us. One of the greatest distractions is social media because you might find yourself spending countless hours connecting with others, meanwhile disconnecting from your partner. One thing my wife says when she's had a tough mental day is, *"I need to disconnect."* In other words, I need to get my mind lost in something meaningless. When she says this, she ends up getting lost on social media for a short period. I don't have an issue with her getting disconnected for a moment because it's only for a moment. For others, here is where the problem lies, we've become so disconnected that we become disconnected from our relationship. You may notice that when we stay connected to the meaningless, we disconnect from what is meaningful. If you transferred the countless hours you spent on social media into your relationship, I wonder how much deeper and connected you would be.

Jesus knew how to disconnect. The Bible teaches us in Luke 5:16 (NLT) that, *"Jesus often withdrew to the wilderness for prayer."* In one moment, Jesus was with the people, and in the next moment He would slip away. Jesus knew He needed rest to recharge and refuel for His next assignment. We need to do the same. Our relationships cannot be effective if we don't learn to disconnect, rest, and recharge too.

Today, my wife and I challenge you to disconnect from what's disconnecting you. We challenge you to fast all forms of social media for one day. Instead of going on social media, we want you to pray and send your partner an encouraging text throughout the day every time you are tempted with a distraction. If the two of you will be in each other's presence today, make sure to spend quality time together without the use of your cell phone. Be sure to journal about your experience and remember, if you want your relationship to be prosperous and effective, don't forget to disconnect from whatever may be disconnecting you from your lady.

Journal below:

Write what you learned today, how it went and what memories were made.

—

CHAPTER NINE

Consumed by Comparison

If there was one thing I disliked growing up, it was going to the doctor. I had a slight case of white coat syndrome. Everything about the doctor's office gave me anxiety except for one thing-measuring myself. You see, when I was a child, I wanted nothing more than to become a professional basketball player. Every time I went to the doctor's office, I would keep tabs on my growth progress. I would then compare myself to my friends growth progress; I like to call this a little friendly competition. Comparing my growth to my friends' growth was all fun and games when I was a child. However, when I grew up, I had to learn to do away with childish things. Unhealthy comparisons don't grow you; they hinder you.

We live in a society full of comparison. Some compare how many followers they have on Instagram or they compare their salaries and accomplishments. Comparison is all around us, but we can't allow it to get in us. As men, we are competitive by nature. But have you ever stopped and wondered why? We can't be competitive without comparison, but the comparison is inaccurate because we are all in a different race. If we are all assigned to a different race, then we all have different measurements that lead to different battles. In the end, we all have different outcomes. If one of your goals with your partner is to move into an upscale apartment and then one of your friends exclaims that he and his wife just purchased their first home, this has the potential to make you feel like you're missing the mark. Of course, this is far from the truth, because you are in a different race. Another couple's success does not mean that you are falling behind because you can't fall behind when you're running your own race.

A passage that moves me and breaks me away from comparing myself to another is Romans 12:15 (NIV) which states, *"Rejoice with those who rejoice, mourn with those who mourn."* This passage teaches us how to celebrate others. When you celebrate others, what you're doing is eradicating the spirit of comparison. When you see another couple accomplish a goal before you do, celebrate them and keep looking forward. When you see another couple has a near *"picture perfect"* child that remains calm in every situation, but yours won't sit still for more than 30 seconds, celebrate them and keep looking forward. When you see that a couple is vacationing at the same place you desire to vacation, celebrate them and keep looking forward. I am encouraging you to do this because celebration is the cure to comparison. You can't live a life of comparison if you celebrate others and keep looking forward.

Today, my wife and I encourage you to process with your lady. Are there any areas in your life that have been consumed by comparison? It could be in ministry, in your relationship/marriage, in your career, etc. We would like for you to write these things down and then destroy them. Rip this list up and throw it away. Then we want you two to declare aloud, *"I am content with who I am, with what I have, and with where I am in life. From this day forward I will find my contentment in Christ and will no longer be consumed by comparison."* Be sure to journal about your experiences and remember that what God has for you will make its way to you. Seek Him daily and allow Him to lead you and your relationship. A personal relationship with Christ will satisfy you and fulfill you more than anything else ever could.

Journal below:

Write what you learned today, how it went and
what memories were made.

—

CHAPTER TEN

Love Keeps Record of Rights

If there's an area that I used to struggle in, it was that I could do 99 things right, but if I made one mistake, I would focus on the one mistake and would allow that one mistake to get the best of me. The reason for it is because I'm a bit of a perfectionist. If things aren't perfect, it stresses me out. What I've realized is that mentality is dangerous. It's dangerous to let one imperfection make me lose sight of everything that's going well for me. I'll allow one thing to hinder my joy because things aren't perfect. The truth is some of us have that mentality when it comes to our relationships. Your partner could be doing 99 things right, but if they mess up on one thing, you'll allow the one thing to blind you from all the other great things your partner does.

I love what the Bible says in 1 Corinthians 13:5 (NIV). It says, *"Love keeps no record of wrongs."* In other words, what Paul is teaching us is that if our relationships are going to be prosperous, then we need to learn to bring up the future and not the past. Remember, it is hard to move forward when you continue to remind your partner of their past mistakes. Too often the reason why we continue to remind our partners of their past is that we want to prove them wrong. Whether you are wrong or right, nobody wins the fight if you're not unified. We need to hold records of rights. When you hold and speak records of rights, you create an atmosphere of encouragement. This type of atmosphere allows your relationship to grow stronger and healthier.

The Bible teaches us that you reap what you sow. If you want your relationship to be fresh and exciting, then you need to sow encouraging seeds into your relationship. Sow into the direction in which you want your relationship to go. If you want your relationship to have more love, sow more love. If you want your relationship to have more grace, sow more grace. If you want your relationship to have more peace, sow more peace. I want you to understand that your harvest will be directly linked to what you sow.

It's time to put to death all records of wrongs, and it is time to move forward into a blessed and prosperous future with your partner by collecting and keeping record of rights. My wife and I challenge you and your partner to create a record of rights. Take 10-20 minutes (more if you need it) to write down a list of everything your partner has done right lately. Then we would like for the two of you to read your list to one another and hug it out. Thank your partner for everything she has done right. Be sure to journal about your experience and from this point forward meditate on her rights and not on her wrongs.

Journal below:

Write what you learned today, how it went and what memories were made.

—

CHAPTER ELEVEN

The Little Things Matter

Have you ever done something you thought was insignificant, but turned out not to be? I'll never forget the day when I went out fishing with my father and friends. I was 13 years old and enjoying life as we boated down the Pacific Ocean. As we patiently waited for a catch, I noticed a small plastic key. I did not know what the purpose of it was, but I did know I wanted to play with it, and that is what I did. After entertaining myself with this key for several hours, I put it in my pocket for safe keeping. Just as we were wrapping up to head home, my dad realized that the boat wouldn't start. He frantically checked the engine to see if kelp had become caught in it, he checked to see if the anchor was up, and he checked the engine key. Everything was fine, but the boat still wouldn't start. We called the coast guard and waited a significant amount of time before I asked my dad if the small plastic key in my pocket would be of any help. My dad replied, *"Son where did you get that?"* I informed him that I had taken it off the dashboard and was playing with it all day. My dad responded, *"That is the emergency lanyard, and we need it to start the boat; let me see it."* He took the lanyard and placed it in its proper position on the dashboard, and to no surprise, the boat started!

It was a little thing I overlooked that made a huge impact. It was a small key, but that key had us stranded until it was placed in its proper position. My question for you is, what little things are you overlooking that are stopping your relationship from moving forward?

Too often we overlook the little things because we think that they don't make an indelible difference. The truth is that's a lie. If a seed has the potential to turn into a forest, if an ember has the potential to turn into a wildfire, I wonder what little thing can ablaze our relationship? I have seen husbands who are so busy trying to give their wife the world but fail to realize the world they want is their husband. There is something wrong with buying your wife gifts if you can't give her the gift of time. If you can't listen to how she is feeling, or make her priority, something's wrong. Don't undervalue yourself, because you is what she wants.

I've been to numerous funerals, and no one ever says, *"I wish I would have bought her more gifts. I wish I would have bought her a car. I wish I would have bought her a house"*. They often say, *"I wish I would have spent more time with her. I wish I would have basked in her presence. I wish I would have listened to her."*

The things we often regret are the little things we often neglect. That's why I am encouraging you to make sure you don't undervalue the little things.

My wife and I challenge you to make the little things in your relationship matter. In doing so, you will keep your relationship fresh and on fire. Give her a massage. After dinner, wash the dishes. Text her with a message letting her know how much you appreciate her. Spend time listening to her. We believe that as you do this the level of honor will raise in your household. Be sure to journal about your experience and make sure you do not overlook the little things because they will always make a big impact.

Journal below:

Write what you learned today, how it went and what memories were made.

CHAPTER TWELVE

—

Wisdom
Seekers

I'll never forget an article I stumbled upon while on my honeymoon. The article was about hidden valuables found in people's backyards. The article showed photos of gold, jewelry, and ancient artifacts that homeowners found while digging in their yards. As I read this article, I thought, *"What valuables do we have in our backyards that we are overlooking?"* I believe there are people in our lives that we haven't dug from yet. The Bible teaches us that a valuable called wisdom exists inside those who are around us.

The Bible teaches us the value of wisdom in Proverbs 16:16 (NIV). It says, *"How much better to get wisdom than gold, to get insight rather than silver."* There is value in wisdom, but are we drawing it out of people? On a consistent basis, my wife and I make sure to draw wisdom from others. We seek wisdom from our pastors, parents and friends who have accumulated wisdom in the areas that we could use guidance in. Why? Because we're not going to reach out for wisdom from people who haven't mastered that area. Far too often what hinders relationships is when people who are married reach out to single people; and we have single people that reach out to other single people. The issue with this is that you're asking advice from someone who isn't experienced in that area. Guidance without experience is just a hindrance to your journey. You need wisdom from people that have conquered the mountain you're trying to conquer.

The dilemma with receiving proper wisdom from others is that sometimes we don't like to hear what they have to say. Simply because we know they may say something contrary to what we want to hear. Something similar happened to the Centurion in the book of Acts. The Bible teaches us in Acts 27 that Paul gave advice to the Centurion about their trip to Rome. He told the Centurion not to move forward in going to Rome because of the severe weather. Instead of listening to the wisdom of the apostle Paul, the Centurion listened to the advice of the captain and owner of the ship, and because of this they found themselves in a shipwreck and lost everything but their lives. One word threw them off course and destroyed the ship. Now imagine if they listened to the wisdom of Paul. They would have saved their ship and their belongings. Friends, wisdom matters. It's better to hear a word that will prevent you from a storm than lead you to it. When someone gives you advice, pray about it and see what the Lord has to say. We need people in our lives that will tell us what we need to hear, even if it hurts us. Truth sets us free, but lies keep us in captivity. Let's be seekers of wisdom.

Today, my wife and I challenge you to become a wisdom seeker. This means you will not try to do life on your own. Find a couple in your life that is living a life that inspires you, and ask them out on a double date. Mentally prepare for this double date by thinking of some questions you would like answered. Make sure your questions are in alignment with the life they are living. If they have been married for 15 years, ask them the secret to their success. Whatever you need wisdom in, seek it from them. After your double date, make sure to journal the wisdom you gained. Remember, *"As iron sharpens iron, so a friend sharpens a friend."* Proverbs 27:17 (NLT) After your double date, you and your lady are going to be sharper, wiser, and stronger.

Journal below:

Write what you learned today, how it went and
what memories were made.

CHAPTER THIRTEEN

—

The Beauty in the Struggle

If there is one thing every relationship has in common, it's that they have all encountered struggle. We might not all share the same struggle, but every struggle we encounter is intended for our journey. Too often we can find ourselves complaining about our struggle rather than embracing it. The greatest gift God could give your relationship is the gift of struggle. The gift of your struggle will make you pray as if your life depended on it. The gift of your struggle will make you lean on your faith like nothing else matters, humble you, and make you realize that without God you cannot do anything. The struggle is a gift, misunderstood until time reveals the beauty of it.

While working for my father's landscaping company, he made me work every winter break, spring break, and summer break. While all my friends were at the beach, I was at work by 5 AM getting ready to do yard work. One day I couldn't take it anymore, and I asked my dad why I had to get up and work every day while my friends played. Why couldn't I have fun and go to the mall, or play ball with the boys? He said, *"Son, one day you will thank me for everything I'm doing for you. You don't understand it now, but one day you'll thank me."* I didn't understand those words at that precise moment, but as life progressed, I soon did. My father wanted the best for me, so he shaped my work ethic. My father wanted me to be blessed, so he shaped my integrity. I didn't understand what my father was doing, but what didn't make sense to me then didn't mean there wasn't value in it. Same goes for your relationship.

The hardships you go through as a couple is not to break you down but to build your relationship up. The struggles you face aren't to make you bitter, but to make you better as a couple. There's beauty in the struggle and eventually time will reveal the beauty to you.

Today, my wife and I challenge you to talk about your struggles with your partner. Maybe the two of you are experiencing financial difficulties or have recently experienced loss or disappointment. We believe that life is not a waiting room, but a classroom because while working toward your dreams, there are many lessons to be learned. We challenge you to make peace with your struggles by finding the beauty in the struggle. Here are a few questions to ask one another: What do you think God is trying to teach us through our present struggle? Do you think you have been allowing God to process you or have you been fighting it? Where do you think our present struggle is leading us? What lessons have you learned from our struggles? Journal your answers, so you have something to look back on when you're walking in the fullness of your dreams, and never forget that there is beauty in the struggle. Romans 8:28 (NLT) promises that *"God causes everything to work together for the good of those who love Him and are called according to His purpose for them."* With that promise in mind, don't worry, don't fear, because whatever battle you may be facing, God is working it together for your good.

Journal below:

Write what you learned today, how it went and
what memories were made.

—

CHAPTER FOURTEEN

L.O.L Love Out Loud

My grandmother used to say to us, *"Don't buy me roses when I am dead. Buy me roses while I am still alive, so that I can enjoy them."* One of the greatest things you can do for your partner is express your gratitude for them; because whenever you compliment your partner, you bring confidence to your partner. Too often we think about the good things that our partner does, but we don't regularly say it. An unexpressed compliment isn't a compliment at all. Whenever a compliment enters your mind learn to speak it out loud.

I love what the Bible teaches us in Proverbs 16:24 (NKJV). It says, *"Pleasant words are like a honeycomb, sweetness to the soul and health to the bones."* This Scripture reminds us that our pleasant words matter. They bring sweetness to our soul and health to our bones. One word can change the dynamic of your partner's heart!

What I love about my wife is she consistently encourages and compliments me. She is my biggest cheerleader. I will never forget the day when I did not want to preach. I was having an off day; I felt inadequate, worn down, and discouraged. When she noticed me, she didn't run with my feelings; she ran with the spirit. She looked at me and said, *"Get up, you are going to preach tonight, and you're going to preach a powerful word. You are called for this, you are anointed, and you are a powerful man of God. The enemy is only attacking you because you are going to win souls for God tonight. So, get up, cheer up, and get ready to be used greatly by God."*

The moment I heard this my soul was refreshed, and my spirit was revived. I went out to preach that night, and the altar was filled. If my wife hadn't expressed those words, I would have had a defeated night. Instead, I got up in victory because of a pleasant word. Her pleasant words, at that moment, changed my life. I wonder how many moments would change in our partner's life if we learned to do the same thing. Encouragement brings nourishment to our lives.

Today, my wife and I challenge you to no longer be silent with your words, because love should never be silent. We challenge you to love out loud by refusing to hold back words of encouragement. Tell your partner the kind things you feel about her. You can do this through text, social media, or in person. If you choose to do this through social media, hashtag #14daychallenge for a potential repost. Be sure to journal about your experience and have fun loving out loud.

Journal below:

Write what you learned today, how it went and
what memories were made.

Thank you!

Thank you so much for joining us on this 14-day challenge. We love the fact that you care enough about your relationship to invest time into it. We hope that you learned more about one another, fell more in love, and grew closer to God during this 14-day challenge.

Each day you had a different challenge, but we encourage you to incorporate the challenges into your daily life so your relationship will continue to stay fresh and on fire.

We can't wait to hear all about your experiences! Hashtag #14daychallenge on social media. We will frequently check up on this hashtag to get to know you and your significant other. Again, thank you for joining us on this challenge.

Love Always,
Rich & Britt

BIO

Richard and Brittni De La Mora live in San Diego, CA. They are the directors of the young adult ministry called the Uprising at Cornerstone Church of San Diego and are the founders of Always Loved. They are evangelists, authors and make YouTube videos. You may have seen them on ABC's The View, CBN's The 700 Club, TBN Salsa, or National Geographic's Drugs Inc. They have a passion for bettering relationships, reaching the lost at all cost, and inspiring all people to live out their God-given potential.

Where to find us online

We love connecting with people on social media, so feel free to stop by and say hi, we would love to e-meet you!

INSTAGRAM

Rich: @Richardelamora

Britt: @Brittnidelamora

TWITTER

Britt: @Brittnidelamora

WEBSITES

Britt: Brittnidelamora.com

FACEBOOK

Rich: Richandbritt

Britt: Brittnidelamora

SNAPCHAT

Username: Brittnidelamora

Made in the USA
Middletown, DE
11 May 2020

93874794R00046